KNOWING YOUR CIVIL RIGHTS

A T R U E B O O K®

by
Christin Ditchfield

Children's Press®
A Division of Scholastic Inc.

New York Toronto London Auckland Sydney
Mexico City New Delhi Hong Kong
Danbury, Connecticut

Signing a petition is a way of exercising one's civil rights.

Reading Consultant
Jeanne Clidas, Ph.D.
*National Reading Consultant
and Professor of Reading,
SUNY Brockport*

Content Consultant
Jonathan Riehl, J.D.
*Graduate Instructor,
Communications Studies
University of North Carolina,
Chapel Hill*

Library of Congress Cataloging-in-Publication Data

Ditchfield, Christin.
    Knowing your civil rights / by Christin Ditchfield.
        v. cm. — (A true book)
    Includes bibliographical references.
    Contents: Do you know your civil rights? — The Bill of rights —
The civil rights movement — Equal rights for everyone —
Respecting our civil rights.
    ISBN 0-516-22800-5 (lib. bdg.)   0-516-27910-6 (pbk.)
    1. Civil rights—United States—Juvenile literature. 2. Civil
rights movements—United States—History—20th century—Juvenile
literature.   [1. Civil rights. 2. Civil rights movements—History—
20th century.]
I. Title. II. Series.
  KF4750.D49 2004
  342.7308'5—dc22
                                                    2003022704

Contents

Civil rights are guaranteed to all U.S. citizens.

Do You Know Your Civil Rights?

It makes no difference whether you are male or female, young or old. The way you look does not matter, nor does your family background or your religious beliefs. As a member of your community, you have the right to freedom and equal

treatment under the law. These are your civil rights.

You exercise your civil rights when you speak out about an important issue or vote on laws that will affect you. Your civil rights give you freedom to attend religious services. They protect your privacy and allow you to defend yourself. **Citizens** of the United States have many freedoms and responsibilities.

Voting is a civil right guaranteed to U.S. citizens who are eighteen years old or older.

When the United States of America became a country, its leaders created a **document** called the Constitution. The Constitution lays out the rules for the American system of government. The first leaders of the United States believed that individual freedom was one of the most important **principles** of government. They wanted to be sure that the new government they were creating would protect

A painting showing United States leaders writing the U.S. Constitution

the rights and freedoms of its citizens.

At first, the Constitution did not specifically list all of these freedoms. This concerned many people. So new laws,

The Bill of Rights

called amendments, were added. The first ten amendments to the Constitution are known as the Bill of Rights.

The Bill of Rights

The First Amendment to the U.S. Constitution guarantees U.S. citizens several liberties, including freedom of speech. Freedom of speech is the freedom to express ideas. It means people may express their opinions in public speeches and **debates**. They can share their

11

Freedom of speech allows people to express their opinions in many different ways.

thoughts in books, magazines, newspapers, movies, music, radio, and television. Freedom of speech even includes "speech acts"—when people show what they think by carrying signs or wearing symbols.

The First Amendment also gives U.S. citizens freedom of the press and the freedom to assemble peacefully. Neighbors can gather together to discuss important issues that affect their community. They can sign **petitions** demanding that unfair laws be changed. Journalists can criticize the government. They can report the news as

A television reporter covering a protest against government policies

they see it, regardless of whether the government approves of what they say.

In addition, the First Amendment grants citizens freedom of religion. In some

14

countries, the government decides what religion its citizens must follow. American citizens may worship any way they please, and they are free to share their religious faith with others.

People in the United States have the right to practice any religion they choose.

The Second Amendment protects the right of citizens to "bear arms," or own guns. The Third and Fourth Amendments protect citizens' privacy. Citizens cannot be forced to house soldiers. The police cannot search a person's home, car, or personal belongings without just cause—without good reason to believe a person is involved in illegal activity. Often, police must get a warrant, a legal document

The Bill of Rights states that the police cannot search a person's property without just cause.

signed by a judge that grants permission for the search.

The Fifth, Sixth, Seventh, and Eighth Amendments all protect the rights of the **accused**. A person cannot be forced to **confess** to a crime.

17

Accused citizens have the right to receive advice from a lawyer. They have the right to a fair and speedy trial. The government may not inflict cruel and unusual punishment on criminals. In addition to the protections of these amendments, American law has always said that a person is considered innocent until he or she is proven guilty.

The Ninth Amendment states that citizens have other rights not specifically mentioned in the Constitution. These rights are just as important. The government cannot pass new laws that take away the rights listed in the first eight amendments.

The Civil Rights Movement

The Bill of Rights became law in 1791. The Constitution guaranteed civil rights to all U.S. citizens. In reality, however, many people were denied their civil rights. Slavery was legal in the United States until 1865. After slavery ended, most African-Americans were still

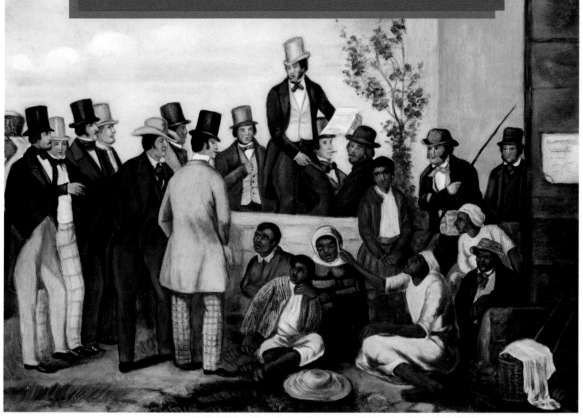

treated differently than whites. Many blacks were not allowed to vote until 1868, when the

Fifteenth Amendment was passed. Even after that, blacks were often prevented from voting.

Almost one hundred years later, blacks were still being treated like second-class citizens. Many communities adopted segregation, the practice of separating blacks and whites. Blacks and whites lived in separate neighbor-hoods. There were schools for black children and schools for

A segregated drinking fountain in the South in the 1950s

white children. Blacks had to sit in the back of city buses. They could not use "white" restrooms or water fountains in public buildings. They were

23

not allowed to enter many stores, restaurants, and hotels. Other businesses forced blacks to use separate entrances or remain in separate parts of buildings, away from white customers. Local laws support-ed this segregation.

The civil rights movement began in the 1960s. All over the United States, people who opposed segregation began **protesting** in the streets. African-Americans organized

During the civil rights movement of the 1960s, people demonstrated for the rights of African-Americans.

boycotts. They refused to ride in segregated buses. They stopped shopping in stores where they were treated disrespectfully. People marched through towns carrying signs and banners. They demanded that unfair laws be changed.

Finally, in 1964, President Lyndon B. Johnson signed the Civil Rights Act. Segregation was no longer legal. The federal government said once and for all that all citizens had

President Johnson hands his pen to civil-rights leader Martin Luther King Jr. just after signing the Civil Rights Act of 1964.

the same rights and privileges under the law, regardless of the color of their skin.

"I Have a Dream"

On August 28, 1963, civil-rights leader Martin Luther King Jr. addressed a crowd of more than 200,000 protesters in Washington, D.C. In his famous speech, King talked about his dreams for the future of the United States. He hoped the day would come when all Americans would be able to enjoy the rights guaranteed to them by the Constitution. King said, "I have a dream that my four little children will one day live in a nation where they will not be judged by the color of their skin, but by the content of their character."

Equal Rights for Everyone

African-Americans are not the only citizens whose civil rights have been ignored. For many years, women were not allowed to own property. They could not attend certain schools and universities. Women could not vote or run for public office. They could

Women demonstrating for the right to vote in the early 1900s

Women have fought hard for the right to enter professions that were once open only to men.

not compete in sporting events, such as the Olympic Games. Women were not permitted to hold certain types of jobs. They did not get paid as much as men did, even when they did the same work.

In 1920, the Nineteenth Amendment gave women the right to vote. Ever since, American women have been working to achieve equality in society: equal opportunity, equal responsibility, equal pay.

In recent years, the U.S. government has passed laws to defend the rights of senior citizens. These laws protect

In the United States, a senior citizen cannot be fired from a job simply because of his or her age.

the elderly from being cheated, mistreated, or abused. Older workers cannot be fired from their jobs or forced to retire simply because of their age.

In 1990, the Americans with Disabilities Act was passed. This law requires schools, restaurants, and businesses to be **accessible** to people with disabilities. They must provide

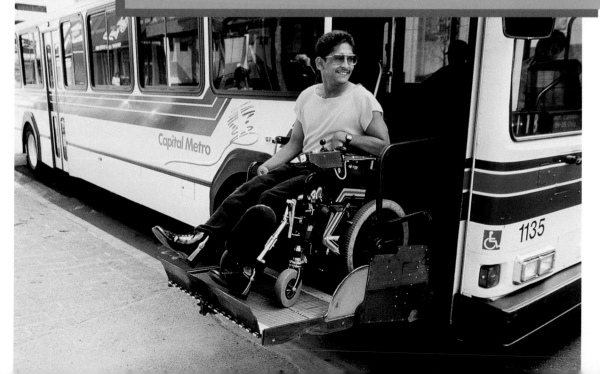

By law, people with disabilities must have access to public transportation. Here, a public bus is equipped with a wheelchair lift.

handicapped parking spaces, wheelchair ramps, and wider entrances and hallways. Employers cannot refuse to hire someone simply because he or she has a disability.

All over the country, students are discovering their civil rights. They exercise free speech by protesting school policies, wearing certain symbols, or writing their opinions in school newspapers. Students who are concerned about their privacy

have objected to locker searches and drug testing. Some refuse to say the Pledge of Allegiance because it includes the phrase "under God." Others insist they have a right to pray and share their faith on their school campus.

"You Have the Right

According to the Constitution, people accused of crimes cannot be forced to confess or admit their guilt. Before speaking to police, they have the right to receive advice from an attorney.

In 1963, a man named Ernesto Miranda admitted committing a violent crime. He escaped punishment, however, because the police had not told him that it was his right to refuse to answer their questions.

Ernesto Miranda

Ever since the Miranda case, police officers have been required to read criminal suspects the Miranda Warning, which advises them of their civil rights.

to Remain Silent"

When an officer makes an arrest, he or she begins, "You have the right to remain silent . . ."

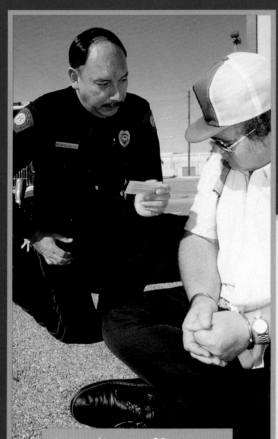

A police officer reading the Miranda Warning during an arrest

Miranda Warning

You have the right to remain silent. Anything you say can and will be used against you in a court of law. You have the right to speak to an attorney, and to have an attorney present during any questioning. If you cannot afford a lawyer, one will be provided for you at government expense.

Respecting Our Civil Rights

It is important for all of us to understand our civil rights. We need to know what freedoms we have and how we can use them. We also need to understand our responsibilities. Just because we are free to do something does not mean that

A woman expresses her views at a town meeting as others listen respectfully.

we should do it. We must use our freedom wisely. While we exercise our own civil rights, we should take care to respect the rights of others.

From time to time, those freedoms will be in danger. The United States has come under attack. Foreign countries have tried to limit or control its freedom. The country's own leaders have sometimes suggested new laws to be added to the Constitution—laws that would take away or restrict civil rights. People need to be alert to the danger. United States citizens must always be ready to defend their country and the freedoms it has given them.

During a Martin Luther King Jr. Day parade, students carry signs thanking Dr. King for his work in helping achieve civil rights for all.

To Find Out More

Here are some additional resources to help you learn more about civil rights:

 **Books**

Ditchfield, Christin. **Freedom of Speech.** Children's Press, 2004.

Duncan, Alice Faye. **The National Civil Rights Museum Celebrates Everyday People.** Troll Associates, 1999.

Pascoe, Elaine. T**he Right to Vote.** Millbrook Press, 1997.

Quiri, Patricia Ryon. **The Bill of Rights.** Children's Press, 1998.

Sobel, Syl. **The U.S. Constitution and You.** Barron's Educational Series, Inc., 2001.

Organizations and Online Sites

Constitutional Rights Foundation
601 South Kingsley Drive
Los Angeles, CA 90005
http://www.crf-usa.org

This site helps young people understand the value of the Constitution and the Bill of Rights.

U.S. National Archives and Records Administration
700 Pennsylvania Ave. NW
Washington, DC 20408
http://www.archives.gov

On this site you can view the Declaration of Independence, the U.S. Constitution, and the Bill of Rights.

The White House
1600 Pennsylvania Avenue NW
Washington, D.C. 20500
http://www.whitehouse.gov

Check out *www.whitehouse kids.gov* for a virtual tour of the White House as well as games, quizzes, time-lines, and historical trivia.

Important Words

accessible able to be used by

accused someone charged with having done something wrong

boycotts acts of refusing to take part in something

citizens members of a particular country

confess to admit to doing wrong

debates discussions between people with different views

document paper containing important information

petitions letters signed by many people demanding change

principles basic rules that govern people's behavior

protesting speaking out against something

Index

Meet the Author

Christin Ditchfield is an author and conference speaker, and is host of the nationally syndicated radio program *Take It to Heart!* Her articles have been featured in magazines all over the world. A former elementary-school teacher, Christin has written more than twenty-five books for children on a wide range of topics, including sports, science, and history. She makes her home in Sarasota, Florida.